ROCKY

The Man with the Mask

GW00655895

ROCKY

The Man with the Mask

Michael Ackermann

HODDER AND STOUGHTON
LONDON SYDNEY AUCKLAND TORONTO

British Library Cataloguing in Publication Data

Ackermann, Michael
  Rocky: the man with the mask.
  1. West Germany. Hamburg. Social life. Biographies
I. Title   II. Rocky, der Mann mit der Maske. *English*
943.5150870092

ISBN 0-340-52458-8

For Kirsten

Contents

Illustrations

Introduction

Sunday morning. 7.00 a.m. Hamburg fish market.

There's a strange face in the crowd, multi-coloured and tattooed all over. Rings through his ears, a ring through his nose. The whole spectacle topped by a Mohican haircut.

Then the crowd parts and you get a full view. It's Rocky the Mohican in his leathers and studs.

Rocky's jacket with its long fringes and hundreds of studs is known all over Hamburg – and beyond – but especially in the red-light district of St Pauli where he has spent most of his life. His old leather jacket and his chains are his trademark, a symbol of power and violence.

The market-goers don't know quite how to react. Then an elderly man with a camera dares to step forward.

"Excuse me, but may I take your photograph?"
His wife is nervous.
"Come on. Let's go, before it's too late!"
But Rocky goes right up to them.
"Sure you can take a photo."
"See," says the man, "he's OK really . . ."
And he's right.
Since then Rocky the Mohican from St Pauli has

hung up his leathers. Hardly anyone knows why. But something has happened. Everyone knows that.

*   *   *

He is lying in a hospital bed now, a thin gaunt man, over sixty years old. At first glance he might seem like any other sick old man, except for the tattoos covering his face and body. And there is something else, too, that draws the continual stream of visitors to his bedside. What is it? Something in his eyes perhaps?

As you hear his incredible story you will find out what has happened from the man himself.

Rocky has never written his story down, though he has told it many times, especially in these last months. Nothing would please him more than to tell it to you.

So pull up a chair to the edge of his hospital bed. Shut out the noise of the busy ward and listen hard – his voice is getting weaker now – to the story of Rocky the Mohican.

Daddy was a Nazi

Hi! My name is Gerhard Bauer – at least, that's my *real* name. I was born on 26th November 1926, the only child of a traditional German army family. In my father's eyes, a man only counted for something if he wore a uniform. He himself was a senior officer in the Town Council. He judged a man solely by his rank. He was always scrupulous, methodical, restrained, a man who showed no emotion. If he bought flowers for Mother he would carry them hidden in a briefcase. Anyone who carries flowers in his hand parades his affections. My old man showed none.

I was a delicate child, and he made me suffer for it. I wanted to be allowed to be happy and sad – to show my feelings. He was bitterly disappointed with his young son. And he didn't hesitate to tell me so.

"They'll never make a soldier out of you," he'd say. Which in father's words meant: "You'll never be a real man."

I tried to prise at least a little affection from him by imitating his obsession with order. I kept my room spotlessly tidy. I lined up my pencils in neat rows. I'd even have lined up the raisins my mother put in her cakes, if only she'd have let me.

The marks of my upbringing are still with me. Even today there's a regimented streak in me. Although I'm very ill now, I like to strut around the Altona and St Pauli districts of Hamburg as if I'm on parade. I observe etiquette with scrupulous precision, always. It gets into the blood, you know. Though, of course, in my time I've hit rock-bottom. But I'll tell you about that later.

Nazi child

In the years that followed the First World War a spirit of freedom swept through Germany. It was the golden age of Jazz and Swing. My father hated it. He retreated into the past. Politically, the mood was uncertain. But early on my father joined the Nazi Party and wore the gold party badge. Most of the neighbours were socialists or communists. His red armband marked him out – a misfit in the Berlin street where I grew up.

As the child of a Nazi I wasn't allowed to play with children my own age. I felt trapped in my own home, locked in a golden cage. I lacked nothing, nothing but a way out. I hardly met other children. I learnt to be alone. I built myself a world of dreams. No-one else knew about it. It belonged to me alone.

Sometimes I could hear the children outside laughing and shouting.

"You're staying here!" my father would say.

Sometimes tramps would ring the door bell. "Idle pigs!" he would yell at them.

"Ah yes," I thought, "but they're free! Living on the edge. Outsiders. I wish I could go with them."

I always respected my mother, though. I suffered with her in her unhappy marriage to this heartless man. Divorce was out of the question, but it wasn't hard to see through the ridiculous façade of their middle-class marriage. They put on a show of harmony. But it was all fake.

Mother spent all her love on me. But this was a constant source of arguments between them. Father criticised her for molly-coddling me. "Spare the rod and spoil the child." Mother didn't agree with his harsh approach. I believe she suffered from it too.

What dignity she had came from her job as a dressmaker. She ran her own business with fifteen employees, which was rare for a woman in those days. I only knew her immaculately dressed, just as I'd never seen my father without a tie on.

Family life revolved around work and the Party. There was no room for the Christian faith in our home. In fact, my father had never set foot in a church, and my mother only went at Christmas and Easter because it was the done thing.

Teachers' pet

In 1932 my mother took me to the "Thirty-Fifth Berlin" secondary school. The sudden contact with other children petrified me. I was desperately shy. If I went home complaining that I'd been beaten up again, I'd get another clout from my father. I found myself becoming a lonely teachers' pet. For "behaviour" I always got an A grade. I had to. Good conduct, attentiveness and diligence were more important than anything to my parents.

I would find the first lily, the first lilac and the first rose of the year and put them on the teacher's desk. If the other children were hatching some practical joke I would leave the classroom with an indignant look. You couldn't fault my behaviour. I'd learnt early on to pretend. You see, even then I was wearing a mask. By the time I was seven I was the class scapegoat. I had to "buy" friendships because I'd never learnt how to make real friends. Pretty soon I realised there are not many people who can't be bought. It's a terrible thing for a child to learn.

I was a thoroughly miserable child. How I envied the children playing in the dirt with their brothers and sisters, dreaming up their games and pranks. It was only later that I found out they'd been equally jealous of me. "Look at him. He gets everything he wants. Spoilt brat!"

Learning to hate

In the year I went into Form Two, Hitler was catapulted into power by the big German industrialists and land-owners. For my parents it was a great victory. They never stopped talking about it. They hung out the flags. We may have been cut off from the neighbours, but at least we belonged to the Party. So it was worth it!

Outside, the masses were starving. Six million unemployed people walked the streets. My parents hung a picture of Hitler in the living room, and every day I decorated it with fresh flowers. It was while I was in Form Two that I gave up any idea of joining the children in the street outside. I realised they didn't want me any more. They didn't even want my presents. No-one wanted to have anything to do with a Nazi child.

Soon the parents of some of those children started to disappear. Those who were socialists or communists vanished into the concentration camps. It was the first year of the Great Dictator.

When I discovered that our neighbour's house-keeper was a Jew I got hold of her daughter and hit her repeatedly, letting out all my pent-up, impotent rage on the girl until I drew blood. The girl's terrified mother begged me not to give her away to my father. Just for a moment, I felt ashamed of myself. In years to come it was my father I was ashamed of.

Escape to the army

I wanted to break free as soon as I could – free from my father, free from home. The main thing was to get out.

When I was fifteen I left school. I got a business apprenticeship with the Berlin *Financial Times*. I didn't care what it was. I'd have been a chimney sweep. Anything to get out from under my father's thumb.

But my uncle was a lawyer on the stock-market. So as an apprentice I still couldn't break free of my parents' control. Because I was my uncle's favourite, the other apprentices cut me off. I was a loner once again.

It was this particular uncle who encouraged me to volunteer for three months' military service. I was seventeen when I became a soldier. It was 1943, and no-one believed any more that Hitler's armies would be victorious. I joined the infantry at Landsberg on the River Warthe.

Becoming a soldier was a kind of penance to appease my father. In my uniform I discovered a bit of self-confidence. It gave me a kind of freedom. In with the other men I felt a sense of belonging. For the first time in my life I was not alone. Even if I was just a small cog in a huge death machine.

But even here I couldn't get away from my childhood habits. I managed to get a special posting by "pedalling", as they called it – crawling to my superiors and treading my inferiors underfoot. I was made an orderly, a boot-boy in the Officers' Mess. Deep down though, I'd rather have roughed it with my mates.

I found myself involved in ambushes in occupied East Germany. I was lost and very frightened. I was trapped by loneliness and the fear of death. Just when I thought I'd finally made it, I was alone again.

God? God never came into it. No-one I knew took God seriously. I knew some Christians, but it was obvious that their belief made no difference to them. I was just trying to survive.

War and captivity

The war taught me that violence was the only way to settle a score. But something in me resisted carrying out-and-out murder weapons. Even later, as a rocker, I swore by blades and chains because they didn't always kill. They always gave a bloke a chance.

The Nazis whipped us up into mass hysteria. "The Führer commands – we obey." Like many young people I was carried along by it right up to the end of the war.

When I was nineteen I was captured by the Americans. A year later, in 1946, I was released. I made my way home to Berlin.

My home was now in the French sector of the town. My father was dead – shot by the Russians in 1945. A callous worshipper of violence to the end, he died with no regrets. My mother had had to give up the house to the French, but was allowed to go on living in a tiny attic room. I was glad to find she had survived at all.

Love among the ruins

A new family moved into the basement. They belonged to the anti-fascist Resistance Movement. I fell in love with their eighteen-year-old daughter. Perhaps our young love was a sign that the deep hatred of the Nazi period that had torn the whole of Germany apart could one day be healed. We both felt misunderstood by our parents. Together we tried to sift through the wreckage of our country and pick up the pieces of our empty lives. We did it to spite our parents, and the post-war poverty we were forced to live in. Inside though, we desperately wanted to make things better between them. We dreamed together of a life of freedom. We got engaged, and soon had a baby daughter. My fiancée worked as a shop assistant. I was unemployed. So again I was dependent – this time on my prospective parents-in-law.

In a last bid to be free I started working for the French, helping people to escape from the Russian occupation zone. It was a highly dangerous job. The Cold War between East and West was just beginning. It was hardly freedom. I was more trapped than ever.

2

Captured

The French authorities were working on a plan to starve the East German economy by draining it of all its "able-bodied human resources", as the official jargon put it. They made me a vague promise that if I did good work for them I would get my parents' home back. I accepted this chance to work for my father's old enemies. My job was secretly to escort workers from the East Berlin mineral mine into the West. The strict selection procedures at the mine guaranteed that the miners were fit and healthy. What the French didn't say was that they were destined to be reinforcements for their Foreign Legion.

I would go into East Berlin disguised as an interested tourist and enthuse about the "golden West", then bring people to West Berlin by train. After a few months the whistle was blown on me. A West Berliner who knew me had been transferred to the East. He'd been watching me for some time. On one trip I was just reaching the border checkpoint when I was confronted by a Russian soldier.

At the start of the fifties

"Hey, you! Come here a minute."

That minute turned into eight-and-a-half years in a labour camp.

I was taken into custody. There was no trial, just interrogations every night from 10.00 p.m. until 5.00 a.m. In the ceiling of the interrogation room there was an iron hook.

"When you've had enough you can always hang yourself," hissed my interrogator.

Very soon they had completely broken and exhausted me.

Life sentence

For weeks I saw nobody except the warders. I was tortured with total isolation. Even the exercise yards were sealed off so I couldn't see the other prisoners.

After some months the Soviet military court passed its sentence: "Labour camp – for life." At that moment, something in me died. But more deaths were to follow.

Russian guards shaved my head. (This ritual humiliation was repeated every four weeks in the coming years.) They took all my possessions away whilst I was in the showers. In return they handed me a threadbare Russian uniform. I was driven through the street of Chemnitz (later Karl-Marx-Stadt) with the other prisoners in an open truck. Passers-by cheered when they saw our uniforms. They thought we were Russian soldiers being brought to justice and imprisonment. How wrong can you be?! Finally, we were taken on to Bautzen, the infamous prison camp in Oberlausitz in the far south-east of East Germany.

Bautzen

Bautzen was a sand-coloured brick-built camp. Its inmates called it "The Yellow Hell". Opposite "The Yellow Hell" was the "Dead Man's Hill", the prison cemetery. Every morning at least ten prisoners' corpses were brought there on a cart.

We lived in barracks about twice the size of a classroom. Up to four hundred men slept in each one. Row upon row of straw mattresses on two levels. If you went out to the toilet in the night you lost your place.

For months we did no real work. If we'd had anything useful to do it would have made us feel more human and kept our morale up. Bautzen was not the worst, I know. Often prisoners were herded on to trains bound for Siberia.

In this endless, meaningless monotony we began to tattoo each other in a primitive way. Some prisoners were tattooed from head to toe. I had two snakes tattooed on my face with the words "Hate" and "Revenge", words which summed up my life for the next ten years. To be tattooed is to be marked for life. But we knew what we were doing. We'd got nothing to lose. We'd finished with our lives.

Bautzen stripped us of everything. Lined up, sack after sack, bed after bed; top army officers next to ballet dancers, opera singers next to factory workers and civil servants. The older ones comforted the younger ones. We turned to each other for some human warmth. It felt good to lie next to a fellow prisoner and feel understood, even for a moment. At night homosexual activity came easily. Inside the prison walls right and wrong didn't come into it. Not when there was someone who would comfort you, wipe your tears away, share his bread with you or give you a bit of floor space. I never felt any shame.

Mother dies

After a year we were allowed to write home for the first time. I told my mother everything that was happening to me. To this day I wish I hadn't. Four months later I was ordered in front of a Russian General. Normally you would have to stand to attention, but he gave me a cigarette and told me to sit down. Two months after receiving my letter, the General said, my mother had suffered a heart attack. By the time the news reached me she had already been buried.

I didn't know how to cope.

I sent my second postcard to my fiancée. I told her I wanted to break off our engagement. I didn't want her to have to wait for twenty-five years. She had her own life to live. She wrote back saying she still felt bound to me. I was encouraged, but also weighed down by her answer. I didn't want to make a second person that I loved unhappy.

*   *   *

The years dragged on. I became very sick with tuberculosis. The "Sick Bay" had no medicine and no doctors, just a few prisoners who tried to nurse each other with nothing but their bare hands. There in the hospital barracks I began to write poetry to stop myself going completely mad. Through my poems I escaped into a world of my own – a spiritual world in which I was renewed. Poetry was the best way, the only way, I could say what I had to say. It was like giving my torturers a slap in the face.

These two poems are part of a whole collection

of writing from the East German prisoner of war camps. I wrote them in about 1953:

Men behind walls and barbed wire

Men behind walls and barbed wire,
Victims of dismal fate,
Sickness gnaws at our bodies,
We cling to our hope and we wait.

We never see flowers blooming,
We never hear children at play,
We see wasted years of night-time,
But we never see break of day.

No justice weighed our sentence,
No laughter lightens the load,
No room for hope in the heaviness,
On this endless cheerless road.

But in spite of it all there is courage,
And a hope to be happy and free,
Though the bloody doctrine is Stalin's,
And we pay the bloody fee.

We may not be mourning much longer,
For the wheel of history turns,
And every wall is blown to the winds,
And every barricade burns.

Our deepest of hopes may be granted,
The hangman may yet find a heart,
And come with a note from the Kremlin,
In time for the mercy to start.

It was only this agonising struggle for survival that kept me going. I pretended to myself that none of this was happening to me.

Driven by despair, I wrote a "Poem against God". Today it makes me weep:

Poem against God

Live? But why should we?
Life is only pain,
Poverty and oppression,
And man alone is guilty of it.

So why do we mock ourselves,
Praying for mercy,
When there is no God to offer it,
Only our own reflection?

And yet some hope remains,
As long as men live amongst men,
So look for hope in a mirror,
Is it you? Is it you?

That was the only spark of hope I had left. My own face reflected in a mirror. Some hope! That's how lonely I was.

From bad to worse

In 1954 Bautzen was taken over by the East German authorities. For the first time it was German warders who were running the infamous prison camp. When the Germans took over things went from bad to worse for us prisoners. The Russians had been unpredictable. But the Germans were just plain heartless. The Russians might have given you a cigarette if they had really bad news for you. The Germans just handed you a telex and gave you a form to fill in.

Our years in prison taught us to expect nothing of life. We learnt to use and abuse each other. We had no respect for ourselves or for anyone else. The struggle to survive poisons people.

Now I've realised that it makes no difference what people look like. It doesn't matter if they're green, blue or yellow. The thing that matters is that we care for each other and look after one another. We've got to stay warm and open with each other and hang on like mad to the things we believe in.

There are still scars left over from my time inside. I can't bear to have any doors locked. Even in my flat I never lock the doors. I'd scream. And I can hardly bear to be alone. The walls start to close in on me. I need fresh air and open countryside and other people wherever I am.

Sudden release

At the beginning of 1957 things began to change. For a start there was no monthly haircut. And all meetings were banned.

Six months went by. Then one night all the lights were suddenly thrown on. Doors banged

open and shut. We heard about twenty men
being called out. Half an hour later the same thing
happened again. This time my name was among
those called. Before I knew where I was, I was
released.

They didn't even let me say goodbye to the
friends I'd spent years of misery with. Those of us
who were being released were lined up and given
a swift haircut and a medical check. Stark naked,
we were herded across the yard to the camp
chapel which was being used as a warehouse. We
were kitted out immaculately. It was like going to
a high-class tailors. From the socks to the hat
everything was a perfect fit. Already they were
calling us "the ex-prisoners".

In total, fifteen hundred men who had been
convicted for alleged spying were given early
release by general pardon of the Soviet Govern-
ment. An international press conference was
held in the Officers' Mess with the freshly-
scrubbed ex-prisoners on display. They told us
what to say, of course. And at the end our former
torturers had the cheek to offer us jobs working
for the East German police force. How come they
suddenly thought so highly of their victims?

A coach took us to the station where we were
each given a ticket for West Berlin and a hundred-
mark note – "Release Money".

I travelled from the transit camp into Berlin and
went to look for my family. I found the woman
who'd promised to love me and stick by me
eight-and-a-half years before. She'd been married to my best friend for four years. Well, what

could you expect? Life's like that. Any remaining faith I'd had in human beings went out of the window.

3

Starting Again

I knew I didn't want to go back to a desk job at my uncle's firm. So I began to train as a nurse at a Catholic hospital in Dortmund. The hospital took me on not out of pity but because I had an official letter saying that I'd been "persecuted in the evil Eastern Bloc".

I'd seen people acting like savages and I'd been betrayed by them, but I was determined not to tar everyone with the same brush. I had to come to terms with my own sense of disillusionment. I thought I could do it by giving help to people who really needed it. I guess I was doing it to help myself more than anyone else.

Training to be a nurse was OK. But as I watched the doctors, nurses and care assistants closely I found I wasn't impressed. Some of them claimed to be Christians, but it didn't seem to make much difference. Sure, they went off to church on Sundays. But they were as self-centred as anyone else. They were arrogant and materialistic . . . only interested in looking after number one. It just added to my contempt for other people . . . and for God.

At the end of my training I went to work in a home run by evangelical Christians in Hannoverschen. There I looked after young people who didn't have much going for them. Some had muscular dystrophy, some had cerebral palsy, others were victims of Kontergan, a drug given to pregnant women which damaged the foetus, causing children to be born without proper arms or legs.

I was in sole charge of seven patients. I had to be everything to them: nurse, parent, friend. By the time I'd dressed them, washed them, fed and cleaned them there wasn't much time for anything else. Anyway, my bosses didn't think that spending time with individuals was important. If I tried to do anything over and above the most basic care the Chief Care Assistant would shout at me: "They come here to die, not to live, you know."

I'd heard that before. It was the same at Bautzen.

Pride and prejudice

I spent most of my spare time taking the young disabled people out. I wanted to give them a taste of life outside the institution. But I soon discovered that "healthy society" doesn't want to be confronted with people in wheelchairs. We couldn't get in to see a show. We couldn't get served in pubs. Shopkeepers sent us elsewhere. I really felt for those young people.

One little boy had no legs. He used to sit on a kind of skateboard and make music. One day I bought him an ice-cream. The next day he arrived on his wheelboard, bringing me a rose.

I was beginning to discover that at the bottom of the heap, amongst people who have been rejected, where life is hardly bearable, you can find genuine human warmth. And where life is easier, where you should be able to expect it, it's not there.

An opportunity lost

In 1960 I met up with some real Christians for the first time. One of the Community Service Volunteers at the home belonged to a Baptist church. I went to the service sometimes, just out of curiosity. I even went on a four-day retreat at Whitsun. There were young people from all over the place. They gave me a welcome like I'd never known before. When they all went home at the end of the four days I felt terribly lonely. It was the same feeling I got time and again in my show business career later in life, when I would leave the stage and go back to my hotel room alone.

But I soon lost touch with the church, when the CSV worker turned his back on Christianity and moved in with a married woman. I cut my ties with the lot of them. Right then I couldn't cope with other people's failures. I wanted to hit out at them and show them up. It gave me an excuse to hate them. I wanted to prove that the Bible was absurd. I wanted to show that Christianity wouldn't work in the real world. I desperately wanted to catch Christians out.

A double life

My first encounter with the church thus came to a sudden end. Every day I had to face the suffering of the people I was caring for, without any inner resources to help me cope with it and with no way of escaping from it. So I started to lead a double life. By day I worked in the hospital, with a normal haircut and make-up covering up my tattoos. By night I swapped my white hospital coat for black leathers and worked as a barman in the "Come Back", a gay night-club frequented by film and TV stars.

I wasn't the only one. Lots of nurses, teachers and social workers, both men and women, went to bars like the "Come Back" at the end of a day's work. All day long they poured themselves out for their clients. At night they were left with a huge emptiness that had to be filled.

Before long, of course, I bumped into people I knew: people with responsible jobs, including church people of various Christian persuasions. They all came to be served by me at the "Come Back". Day in, day out, they played the role of the decent, upright citizen. At night they threw off this burden. I was disgusted by them.

Soon I got promotion at the "Come Back". My job was to recruit rent-boys for the club's VIP customers. In all that time I never met anyone who wasn't wearing a mask, who had a care for anyone but themselves. I was very tempted to expose these hypocrites, especially the Christians. Later in life I was shocked to discover that I was no better than the rest of them.

The sack

In 1964 my boss at the nursing home died. He had been patient and kind to me but his young successor soon had me up in front of the management.

"I have nothing against tattoos, of course," he said, "but they disrupt the working environment."

It was my notice to quit.

Patients and colleagues did all they could to keep me there. The patients trusted me. I was the person they were closest to. They even presented a petition to the home's administrators – but without success. So that was that.

I loved my job helping others. And it helped me, too. But I was too hurt to try for another job. I was afraid my fragile self-esteem would collapse altogether. I knew I was being treated unfairly but I was too weak inside to fight it. The emotional hurts I'd suffered in growing up and in the prison camp hadn't healed completely . . . and they were soon to be torn open again.

4

The Mask

I was alone again. I was desperate for friendship, for people who'd stand by me, people I could rely on. But there was nobody.

I decided I couldn't just sit on my backside, so I went out and bought myself a powerful motor-bike to give me some freedom. Then I decided to have an expert complete the tattooing that had been started in Bautzen. I knew how useful it was to wear a mask. So I went to Hamburg and found an artist who created masks for television. He also did tattoos for private clients. This time I had my whole body tattooed. I told him I didn't want an inch of skin left blank. It cost me three grand.

Now people stared at me in shock. They stared when I walked into a café to order a hamburger or a coffee. The effect was perfect.

Meeting this tattooist opened up a whole new world to me, a weird mix of alcoholics, sexual perverts, media people and Hell's Angels. At first I had doubts about the new company I found myself in. I was afraid I might not survive in the world of organised crime with all its unwritten rules. But I plunged in at the deep end anyway, ignoring the voices inside that were telling me to steer clear.

Rockers' revenge

Soon I was invited to join eight men and four women who had their own rock band. They were planning to camp out for a weekend on the banks of the River Elbe. They were people who had nothing to lose and they didn't ask any questions. They just accepted me as I was. They stuck two fingers up to the world. I could lie around in someone's arms all day, and it was no big deal. All of us had tattoos. We all wore leathers. And we all hated foreigners, especially Turks.

On our weekend away the thirteen of us lay around the camp-fire, getting stoned out of our minds. We made a hell of a racket. A few hundred yards away some Turkish young people were also camping out on the sand. Our noise kept them awake, so at about one o'clock they lobbed some stones over to make their feelings known. The response was immediate. These people I'd spent a quiet day with suddenly let rip with knives, iron bars and chains. I didn't know what to do – whether to give up my new friends or fight with them. In the end I decided to go after them and began shredding the Turks' tents and hitting out at the least provocation. The Turkish youths abandoned their tents and ran for their lives, blood dripping from their knife wounds.

At about 6.00 a.m. two policemen arrived and asked to see our ID cards. They looked like a couple of country bobbies who were dead scared. When even the police are frightened of you there's nothing to stop you. After that I wasn't afraid of anyone in the gang. No-one could touch me now. I'd found my place.

Sold to Satan

The next day the rock group asked me if I wanted to go through their initiation ceremony. The condition was that I agreed to give myself to the power of Satan. I had to sign my life over to the devil. After the initiation test two five-point stars were tattooed on my face. They were a secret sign meaning: "I am God. I heal myself by the power of Satan."

The group, like many rockers today, were into the occult. They celebrated black masses, worshipped skulls and wore upside-down crosses round their necks as a sign of their belief that Satan had defeated Christ. I asked to be a member and was soon wearing the official "robes" – leather gear that was a sort of anti-priest's vestments. As I gave myself up to the group, body and soul, I discovered a new identity. If anyone had suggested to me that I was in danger I would have told them that I knew what I was doing. I thought I was strong enough to deal with anything that came up. I really believed that I was in full control of things as long as I was simply myself.

Even so, I soon found myself doing things that I didn't actually want to. If I was hurting inside I would beat someone up. Easy. But there were moments when, as I was holding a bloke on the floor and grinding my heel into his face, I suddenly realised what I was doing, and I felt sick. It was as if there was someone else doing it. I realised then that there were forces outside of me controlling me. I became ruthless. I gave myself up totally to the group and to the power behind it: Satan himself. I was a hell-raiser, born to make the greatest possible chaos.

Rocky the Mohican

I ditched all the values I'd grown up with. I turned my back on my old self and became someone else. I even got a new name. They called me Rocky the Mohican because my hair was cut in a plume like the Mohican Indians. I felt great in my scruffy leathers. I only washed once a month, and I was proud of it. Skeletons, skulls and chains hung round the walls of my room.

I soon got promotion in the group hierarchy. Like all my fellow-fighters I had "Rocker" tattooed on my left hand and then I had "Roc-Ko" tattooed on my right hand. It stood for "Rocker-Kommandant". In the days that followed we got into all sorts of stuff – big break-ins, robberies, and GBH (grievous bodily harm). Sometimes we left people dead.

Then I got arrested.

In custody I found the other prisoners treating me like a hero, like I was someone to copy. I liked that. Then when it came to my trial the judge gave me a surprisingly light sentence because of my time in Bautzen. I got off with just two years' probation. He said that eight-and-a-half years in prison camp had scarred me so much that this was "bound to happen".

He made a big mistake. It was nothing short of a free ticket to do more violence.

Man of violence

I needed money but I no longer had to ask where it would come from. It just flowed in my direction. When I was at the station once some people pushed money at me out of sheer terror. I breathed violence. In fear and trembling, passers-by held out their wallets, rings and watches, saying, "Here, take this . . . only please don't touch me."

My friend Günther will give you a pretty accurate impression of what I was like at that time. He's the son of a prostitute and until recently he was a pimp, a gambler and an alcoholic. Now he works for the Salvation Army:

> If I saw him on the street I used to give him a wide berth. The name Rocky meant violence. He stopped at nothing. He had the best connections in all the big underworld circles, whether it was pimps, killers or dealers.

> *Günther*

Don't be deceived by the smiles here

We had our own set of rules governing relationships. It was the age of the "new morality", and we took it to its limits. Relationships between men and women were about instant sex, not a life together. None of us asked for friendship or love because we had nothing to give in return. You treated your temporary partner like an object, and you expected to be treated just the same. We were just on the take.

In the end I couldn't see the trouble I was getting myself into. I was so caught up in it that I couldn't see I was on the edge of a precipice. It took people who were right outside the situation to help me, people who could hear my cries for help, muffled and disguised as they were. I can tell you now that when you're sinking in a bog you can't pull yourself out. You can try calling out for help, but what's the point if no-one can hear you?

5

Hypocrites

In the summer of 1974 I started playing gigs in small night-clubs all over Germany. I stopped over in Cuxhaven where I made friends with a pastor's son. I was invited into his home, and the family seemed to take it for granted that I would stay a while. The pastor was a liberal-minded sort of bloke but, boy, he'd had some heartaches from his family. His oldest son had disappeared to join the Red Army Faction, a terrorist group in the Rheinland; his third son was very musical but had been forced to learn a trade, so he'd turned against his father; the fourth, who was still at school, was a real rebel. Only the second was following his father in studying theology.

This family was a puzzle to me. I couldn't work them out. They seemed to have so many problems. I couldn't figure out why a man with so much on his plate would still want to talk about Jesus. He criticised my skull-and-crossbones symbols but his words just bounced off me. I just felt like he was wagging his finger at me. It might have been more credible if the pastor had been a bit more honest about his own shortcomings and inadequacies. But I just had the impression that he wanted to do a good deed – and I didn't want to be on the receiving end. I sank back in my old mire, even more convinced that Christians were a load of hypocrites.

Back in Hamburg I got to know Theo, a bloke who did tattooing as a hobby. He and his wife took me into their home without any questions. Theo was a compulsive drinker, but there was always a bed free at his place, even for me.

A few weeks later I got invited to a church. I went to a service. But people stared at me as if I was an alien. I felt like an outcast – like everyone wanted to pray for me but nobody wanted to touch me in case they caught something. I couldn't cope with it at all. I don't know why, but I felt I had to get out of there. Perhaps it was because of the satanic ties I still had. But then I suppose I still had the same satanic ties when I did finally respond to the gospel. So it wasn't that. It wasn't the message that was wrong either, or the God they tried to tell me about. I guess they just weren't the people God had chosen to get through to me. I was a tough nut to crack!

Kurt

A few months later, whilst I was at Theo's, I met a distinguished-looking older man called Kurt. He was dressed in leathers and asked Theo for a bottle of brandy as soon as he arrived. He seemed concerned at me staying at Theo's and the following lunch-time he invited me over to his flat in East Hamburg. He lived in a first floor, three-bedroomed flat in a brick-built apartment block – Block C. The flat was immaculate, ornate, even a touch overdone in its decor. He suggested that I move in straightaway.

Kurt was a lonely, ageing man who just wanted to make his last years more pleasant and help a few people on the way. He encouraged me to register at the local police station and to lead a more ordered lifestyle, in return for which he would give me a home. It was a golden opportunity.

Over Kurt's living-room door there was a wooden plaque with the word "Abstain" printed on it. He was a homosexual. So I knew what the sign meant straightaway and I respected him for his convictions. It was quite a while before I found the strength in myself to withstand the various temptations I came across in Hamburg, where all kinds of sexuality were in vogue. But I felt increasingly secure with Kurt. After a while I was even calling him "Dad", just in fun.

Kurt had friends at the Hamburg Studios of the NDR (the North German Broadcasting network). They were intrigued by the close relationship between us and sent a camera crew round to interview us. The sign saying "Abstain" was big enough for the camera crew to notice. They commented on it, and seemed amazed at the possibility of anyone being homosexual and yet not sexually active.

Through this contact I was invited to take part in a chat-show called *Three Minutes Past Nine* hosted by Wolfgang Menges. We talked about the prejudices people have against tattoos. I had a lot to say about that, of course. A big record company (Teldec) saw the show and wanted me to make a record. I had to laugh. I couldn't sing – well, only in the bath or when I'd got a few pints inside me. I told them so, but they still wanted me to do it.

Cut the crap

I went to the recording studio and met Ulf Krüger, who wrote the lyrics for a well known singer. He agreed to write some songs for me, but said he wanted to get to know me better first. So he came round to Kurt's flat, and before we knew it he'd moved in. He shared our flat and our lives for a while. Then he wrote two songs for my first record as "Rocky the Mohican". The title song was "Gis a job". It's about the time I was sacked from the Home in Hannoverschen. The song on the B side goes deeper. It's about the way I saw the needs of the people around me and how I wanted to tear the masks off their fat rich faces. You can read it for yourself. It's called "Cut the Crap"!

Cut the crap

My old man used to say,
You gotta find your own way,
Well it ain't worked until today,
So I'm throwin' it away.

When I went to school,
Had to keep the golden rule,
They said long hair isn't cool,
Threw the long-hairs outta school.

The times they may have changed,
But people stay the same,
Even kids can't hack it,
If you wear a leather jacket.

So I say "Cut the crap",
Yes I say "Cut the crap".

I'm not the kinda jerk,
Who does normal kinda work,
With a car and kids and spouse,
And a fully furnished house.

If that's what you call normal,
Then what does that say
For the wops and turks and niggers,
And the drop-outs and the gays?

Man, it would be great,
If we gave each other space,
To be different, to be free,
To be who we wanna be.

So I say "Cut the crap",
Yes I say "Cut the crap".

The record was launched in Hamburg's
trendiest disco, "Trinity". Kurt, my "Dad", was
very proud. I had everything to thank him for.

Soon after the launch party Kurt was taken into
hospital. It was cancer. For ten months I nursed
him. Every night he fell asleep in my arms. One
day he asked if he could take communion. I

couldn't believe it. I'd deliberately rejected everything to do with Christianity. Now I watched in
amazement as the old, dying man took it all on
board. Kurt, my friend, my dad, a Christian!
The last few days of Kurt's life made such an
impression on me. I still think about it today.

At Kurt's funeral the minister didn't even ac-
knowledge me. When it was all over I was left
with the most terrible emptiness inside. I thought
about suicide. I lost about one-and-a-half stone
in weight. Not surprisingly, I became ill with
tuberculosis – the disease I'd had in Bautzen.

I went to hospital in north Hamburg. After a
thorough examination they told me that as well
as TB I had cancer of the bone and prostate. It
was far worse than I could ever have guessed.
They said my spinal column was in danger of
collapsing.

I was given a course of intensive radiotherapy,
with the result that I couldn't hold down any
food. Then I had a prostate operation. Even after I
was discharged I bled continually for a time. As I
was standing on the train, blood soaked through
my trouser leg and ran down into my shoe. I was
in agony. I was like a walking medicine cabinet. I
was afraid of being alone and terrified of dying. I
looked for something or someone to take Kurt's
place. I found it in drugs and the rock music
industry. When I was on stage I'd have
thousands of people screaming for me. But half
an hour afterwards I was alone again.

"And so I said 'Cut the crap'."

6

Sold to the Media

It was a long time ago that rock star Udo Lindenberg and I first bumped into each other. We hit it off straightaway. Udo dedicated his song "So What?" to me. We lost touch because I wasn't listed in the telephone book under "Rocky"! Then one day Udo noticed that our records were put out on the same record label and arranged to meet up again. I remember being strangely shy and reserved when we met. He wanted to sign me up for a tour. I finished some small film parts I was doing and then went on tour with him.

Udo's a sensitive bloke. He's got a heart for people in trouble. He's not just the clown he appears to be when he's on stage. He gets really overwhelmed by the kind of suffering some people have to go through.

But the business has more than its fair share of prejudice and intolerance too. Because of the way I looked not many of the TV presenters even gave me a fair introduction. In show business those who've already made it big don't want to know you if you're still struggling to get on the first rung of the ladder.

Once I was with Udo everyone treated me differently. The bank manager, who'd shown me the door up till now, suddenly wanted to offer me a personal loan! Neighbours from Altona, the working-class part of Hamburg, asked me when I was going to move to Blankenese, the posh end of town. My friends in their tattoos and leathers seemed to be getting further and further away from me, even though they'd gladly have been seen with me and shared a bit of the limelight.

As a member of Udo Lindenberg's Panik-Orchestra

My recent experience had taught me that fame wasn't all it was cracked up to be. If any young person thinks that the rock industry is all glamour, if they think the sun shines all day, and you're always mixing with interesting people, I have to tell them that they're totally mistaken. For me the glamour only existed during the few minutes of the performance when the fans were going mad and screaming "Rocky!". It was like a drug. To draw thousands under your spell for a few moments is a great kick – what power! But it's an illusion. People wanted me. They loved me. But nobody knew me. Afterwards I felt as abandoned as ever, like I was the loneliest person in the world. No-one could take away my fear of being left alone. It was getting worse each day. And I didn't know anyone who could help me.

Hooked

It wasn't long before I just wanted to run away – to jack in the performances and break off the tour. I spent more and more of my time shut away in my dressing-room. Udo, who was in charge of the tour, asked a famous rock singer for her advice. Her solution was to fill me up with hard drugs. After all, "the show must go on" whatever the cost.

A quarter of an hour after my first shot of heroin I gave my best performance ever.

At first the shots were delivered free of charge or at a "special price for a friend". Then things changed. Soon they were swallowing up all my earnings. The drug scene and rock music are bound up with each other at every level. There, where life is a fast and furious game, loads of people just get pushed from one drug to another. Another potential addict gets welcomed with open arms, just as the devil gloats over the capture of another poor soul. And the dealer, like the devil, knows how to charge.

I couldn't fight against it any longer. When I was on stage I gave myself totally into the devil's hands. I tell you, with Satan's help I could turn a rock concert into a hell-hole, whether in Essen, Frankfurt or Munich. In a few minutes I could get people going till they were acting like demons. Heavy rock, where you can't hear the lyrics any more, is lethal. You're letting someone else take over control.

On the road

Don't get me wrong: during all this time I did know a bit about God. But he was miles away from me, sitting far off in his heaven. What I didn't know about – what I needed to know about – was Christ, who had died on the cross and beaten the devil and fought with death and won. Without knowing about him there was no escape. So I was still left hungry for something more.

One tour followed another. Then there were films, television appearances. I did performances at the classy discos of Kiel and Düsseldorf. Each twenty-minute show earned me five hundred quid.

Even amongst the TV stars at the Hamburg Studios I was a one-off, an original. I remember once someone took out a handkerchief, spat on it and tried to rub my tattoos off. They thought it was all just fancy make-up! They got a shock when they found out it was for real.

A bunch of musicians went with me from bar to bar, getting a kick out of playing gigs with a Hamburg trademark. They weren't interested in Gerhard Bauer. They couldn't care less for me as a person. They were just playing with the bloke in the mask. No-one was interested in what went on behind it.

Once, just once, I told people what I really thought. It was at a benefit concert for cancer research organised by Mildred Scheel, the wife of the former German president. There were rows and rows of VIPs there, all "Mr Squeaky Cleans". So I told them the truth to their faces. I told them there was a hell of a lot more vice and violence hiding away behind their dinner jackets and bow-ties than ever there was behind leathers and studs. Then later I told them about Bautzen and St Pauli. I said: "there the conditions were lousy, but here it's the people who are."

The exhibitionist

After a few years in the entertainment industry I was beginning to be all the things I had most despised. I was only interested in myself. I talked about myself all the time, told the same old stories again and again. I just loved to shock people. I used to think I was "it". Until someone made the slightest criticism . . . then I went to pieces.

A lot of people backed off, I know. They couldn't handle me being so unpredictable; one moment friendly, the next mouthing off. Sometimes I acted like a caged animal, at others like a spoilt child. I was an exhibitionist, always on the look-out for new ways to grab people's attention. I was terrified of not being noticed. It was getting worse, and people could see it.

To anyone outside I looked no different from any of the other small-minded bourgeois people I loathed. I was intolerant, over-sensitive and touchy. By the end I was so like them I was almost respectable. Before I knew it, the advertising industry had hijacked my image, and even the Hamburg Tourist Office was using my picture in their full-colour brochure. They made me out to be a cross between the Hunchback of Notre Dame and the Last of the Mohicans. I'd become a tourist attraction, a symbol of Hamburg's respectability.

1984 saw the climax and the end of my rock career. Udo rang me up. He wanted to take me on tour again. He was making a new record called "Life" and he wanted his latest album, "Götterhämmerung", to be released in Berlin, with him dressed as the Pope, a couple of prostitutes as nuns and me dressed as the devil himself. After a TV recording in Hamburg this unholy crew piled on to the record company's bus and headed for Berlin. But this ultimate freak-show had to be abandoned halfway through. I collapsed and couldn't go on. Cancer had finished me off. I was taken to hospital but the doctors didn't think I had much hope of surviving.

Two Days of Panik in Berlin

The Panik Concert: Udo Lindenberg, Helen Schneider and Rocky

The hell raisers are comin' and they're rockin' and rollin' all over Germany. On 17th September Udo Lindenberg and his Panik Crew will be stoppin' off for a guest appearance at the New World Club, Hasenheide. And since the gig is already a sell-out the hell-raiser and his crew have extended the tour at short notice and will be rockin' at The Spree on 18th September as well.

Udo's 1980 set is chock-full of his biggest hits and Germanised rock 'n' roll oldies. Guesting on the tour are Helen Schneider, the thirty-four-year-old songstress from the States, and Hamburg's own outrageous Rocky the Mohican. The gutsy-voiced Schneider has her own twenty-minute set and couples up with Udo for "Baby, when I'm Down". Rocky, decked out in leathers and tattooed all over, sings the German version of Tim Curry's "I do the Rock" from his twelve-inch single "Gis a Job". Lindenberg's tour is a must.

From the *Berlin Morning Post* (17th September 1980)

7

Hey, Wait!

They discharged me from hospital but the cancer was eating away at my body. I went home. My flat seemed empty now. The four walls seemed to close in on me. The loneliness was unbearable. As often as I could I left the flat and went downtown to the Kiez at St Pauli. That was my real home. I felt I'd be understood there. My flat in Altona was just a place to sleep.

One Saturday evening in June 1985 I was out on the town, looking mean in my chains and studs – ready for trouble, ready to make some, too. I crossed Hamburg Hill and strode down the Reeperbahn as far as Altona Station, every stride calculated for maximum effect.

As I was crossing the station concourse I noticed some mime artists with their faces painted white. There were often street artists there during the summer. I stopped to take a look. It was a group called Youth with a Mission doing a show called *The Lamb*. As soon as I twigged that it was a Christian drama group, I turned to make straight for the station exit.

I didn't want to have anything to do with them. But then a woman from the group shouted after me.

"Hey, wait! We'd like to talk."

"Look out Rocky," I thought. "Time to get outa here!"

I turned to leave and walked straight into a guy with a rucksack on his back. He hailed me warmly.

"Hey, it's good to see you."

I tried to think where on earth I'd seen this guy before. Perhaps he was someone from one of the tours. After all, far more people knew me than I knew people. He put his hand on my shoulder and spoke to me again:

"Hey, you must be pretty cut up to be going round got up like that. You must be hurting inside something bad!"

I couldn't work out how he could know all that. How could he see through my mask? In all these years no-one else had been able to. No-one had ever spoken to me like that before.

By the time I'd got over the shock and realised that this guy belonged with the very people I'd been trying to avoid, it was too late. With a history like mine I wasn't in a hurry to pour my heart out to anyone. But we swapped addresses anyway.

Interestingly, it turned out that this guy, Hans, had only been in Hamburg a day and had no idea who I was. He told me later that he'd not set out to grab some weird-looking bloke, and that if he'd actually been trying to find the famous Rocky he'd never have talked to me like that. He just saw this old rocker who looked like he was crying out for life. Funny, really. It took someone who knew nothing about me, who hadn't even seen me on the telly, to have this amazing insight into what was really going on inside me.

Heinz, another Christian from this group who'd watched our conversation, admitted later:

"If you'd told me that this guy would come back to your house, I'd have said you were cuckoo."

How wrong can you be?

In that brief meeting on the Altona Station Hans pushed a small leaflet into my hands. I escaped at the first opportunity and ran like mad. I glanced at the piece of paper. It had "Meet Jesus: God's Truth" written across the front. I read it with mixed feelings, then threw it away. I didn't want to get involved with Christians again. I could remember the last time.

Turning point

The following day I was walking my usual route down the Reeperbahn to Altona Station. I was wearing my black leather gear. When I got to the station a sad sort of feeling came over me.

"See," I thought to myself, "one day you have a good conversation. The next day they're gone. No-one there. They've cleared off like all the rest."

I'd scarcely finished these thoughts when two young blokes appeared in front of me. They called me by my Christian name.

"Hi! Gerhard."

Just like that. Well, that shook me. That put me straight on my guard. No-one called me that. Didn't they know I was Rocky the Mohican? I hadn't a clue who they were. They'd got one up on me.

"You won't recognise us," they said. "Yesterday we were made up and doing street theatre."

I couldn't believe it. I'd just cursed them and written them off and there they were again. We had another good chat like the day before. All this conversation was doing my chaotic heart good. They invited me to drop in at the Café Augenblick sometime.

A couple of days later I went, just out of curiosity, to find where the café was.

The Café Augenblick was owned by an organisation called the Jesus Centre. It was set up as a drop-in for young people, people who were unemployed, drug addicts, people wanting advice, and so on. Here, the workers from the Jesus Centre met up with people who needed practical help or who just wanted to chat.

As I went inside Hans came up to me. We sat at one of the tables for an hour or so talking. This guy must have had time on his hands. There I was, Rocky the Mohican, from the world of criminals, pimps and prostitutes, heavy metal and the occult. It was weird. I wasn't hostile. I didn't brag about myself as normal. In fact, I was almost shy. I couldn't get over how open our conversation was. For once, I didn't have to put on an act. There was no point if I was going to get anything out of our meeting. Hans wasn't one of those flash, all-mouth Christians who really put you off. This time I couldn't knock him, couldn't just give myself a pat on the back and then head straight back to my old life. I think he was amazed to find that behind the leather jacket and the words and pictures tattooed all over my body there were actually some feelings. And there was fear, too – fear of being abused again.

Hans invited me up to his room. I had to force myself to go with him. I knew something new was beginning. I knew it as soon as I'd heard those people using my real name.

Accepted

Upstairs, Hans asked me if he could pray for me. I wasn't concentrating too well. But I felt somehow that I'd never met this kind of Christianity before. It was as if an angel was speaking to me, and speaking about me to God. For five hours Hans wrestled with God. For five hours I fought with my old self. It was "Gerhard versus Rocky". Hans showed me from the Bible where I'd gone wrong. I knew that addiction of any kind – be it heroin, rock music or sex – could never satisfy me. It only made my need greater. I knew, too, that my dependency would grow until one day it would finish me off. For someone like me who's close to throwing their life away anyway because it's got no meaning any more there are only two alternatives: Jesus or "the golden shot", an overdose of heroin straight into the bloodstream.

Hans asked me if I was ready to kneel down with him. No way! I wasn't going to kneel, ever, and especially not in front of witnesses. Hans knelt anyway and prayed for me. I tell you, I didn't miss a word. This man pleaded with God for me. He asked God the Father to save me. I was fifty-eight years old and for the first time in my life I heard a prayer that cut deep into my heart. An hour later I found myself kneeling beside Hans, praying "Lord, if you can salvage something from my messed-up life, take it."

And the Lord took it.

After I'd prayed I took off my twelve rings and my ten earrings and laid them on the table.

A new home

I decided I wanted to go to a church service and Hans gave me the address of a Baptist church in Altona – 38 Daimler Street. The following Sunday I waited outside my flat, dressed in a black suit, for someone to pick me up. People who walked by laughed. Rocky in a shirt and tie!

The person from the church was late. I kept on waiting. I could feel people staring.

When I was finally picked up, the journey to the service seemed to go too quickly. I was afraid of what might happen. As I got out of the car I

Rocky in a shirt and tie!

could feel two forces tugging at me: a very strong
one behind me pulling me back and another in
front pulling me into the church.

Don't get the wrong impression. Don't think
that suddenly everything was hunky-dory now I
was up off the floor. Two opposing forces were
battling it out over me. The Evil One still had
power over me because of all my old connections
with Satanism, but I felt like someone else was
with me now. Someone new had possession of
me.

I was plagued with the fear that people would
reject me and criticise me. Yet I felt myself sud-

denly surrounded by love. I was quite overwhelmed by the welcome and when the guests
were introduced at the beginning of the service I
said, "I don't feel like I'm a guest here. I think I've
found a home."

A new family

In spite of my reputation the old, faithful believers in this church took me to their hearts with
no questions asked. Retired deaconesses, the
venerable old preacher and Sunday school
children alike showed me affection. This wasn't
human love, but the love of God himself. Only
God's love could do it. Outrageous love for an
outrageous person. They accepted me just like
anyone else. But I know they were wondering
whether I would be able to stand losing the status
I had as a star on the Kiez.

The next Sunday they greeted me as if I'd been
there for years – not as a newcomer but as a
brother. But I quickly noticed that there was
something different in other church members
that wasn't in me. They could express their joy so
spontaneously. When they sang and when they
prayed they were totally caught up in it all. I just
stood there like a pudding – heavy and uncertain,
a bit sad in spite of all the joy of my new start
in life. I wondered if there was still something
keeping me apart from God.

A new identity

The next day I was sitting in the Café Augenblick again. I went there every day but this time Frank, who was the manager of the café, was waiting for me. He told me that I needed to bring everything from my old life to the foot of the cross. He called it a life confession, like clearing out all the muck from my life, not only the big stuff but all the little things too. Every link with the darkness had to be broken off.

For the next twelve days I sat at a table in my flat and wrote. I filled page after page. I wrote down everything that tormented me, everything that weighed me down, every offence against other human beings that I could remember. It hammered home to me how guilty I was in front of God and other people.

Two days after that I made an appointment at the Jesus Centre. I poured everything out to God in prayer. While I was doing this the power that the darkness had over me was so vivid that I nearly collapsed. Then my new friends burnt my written confession. I was only beginning to grasp what this meant. Because Jesus had taken all of it on himself on the cross my whole list of sins could be thrown into the fire. Do you understand? It's mind blowing! He loved me even after all I'd done! As I started to understand it something inside me took flight. Bit by bit I was being set free.

At the next service the church members came up to me in amazement.

"Gerhard, what's up with you? You're so different. Your eyes, your whole face has changed."

I knew why it was. I'd stopped being Rocky. So I could answer them with a free heart: "Jesus has won the victory!"

I was beaming so much I couldn't hide it. The tattooed outside and the free person inside must have made a strange combination.

I began to live with the church members, my new-found family. I got involved with a missionary project working with young punks. It was a good opportunity to meet people who were just like me – or rather just like I used to be.

8

Learning to Let Go

I went to home-group meetings where I learnt more about my faith. And I grew as a Christian in the quiet times I spent with God.

One of the things I found hard to learn – and I guess I still haven't learnt it completely – is how to let go. I lost a lot of good friends when God called me, and of course I was fast losing my own life through my illness. I felt all these things very deeply. I may have been strong when I was on the Reeperbahn but now I was much more vulnerable.

I guess all Christians find it hard to let go of people they've come to love. But it's all part of being a "fisher of men", as Jesus called his disciples. For instance, you get to know someone at an open air meeting or through a conversation and you go with them in their first few steps of faith – but then you have to let them go it alone.

I still found all sorts of relationships difficult, because I was so hypersensitive. And they brought up lots of spiritual questions for me. You see, for someone as old as me there were so many things to work through. The Holy Spirit wasn't going to change me overnight. Instead it happened bit by bit, with a lot of setbacks in between. I guess that was important for me. Otherwise I might have become the same extreme sort of character that I'd been before. Becoming a Christian is just the beginning, as everyone just starting out with God has to learn. That's when the real work begins, working against self-centredness, pride, misplaced self-confidence; against always wanting to be the centre of attention, being mean spirited and drifting back into your old ways.

Just like I'd become a trophy to be shown off by the business-minded community in the Reeperbahn, I was now the pride and joy of a no less efficient Christian fellowship.

It takes a lot for a fellowship to lead someone like me into freedom. My Christian friends had to go a long way with me. They had to challenge my self-centredness again and again, put up with my lies, pay off my debts, give me money for clothes, buses and food, and cope when I let them down too. They had to sort out the truth from the fantasy in the things I told them. And always, always they had to be straight themselves. They had to find ways to lovingly put me right. They had to go back to the Bible day after day to work out how to handle me. That was vital. So you can see that it wasn't just me that changed. The church people had to change too.

The church I belonged to had been welcoming people like me since the early 70s when they

started working with the Jesus Centre. Basically,
they'd stopped forcing people to fit the mould of
the majority of church-goers. They did it on the
basis of what Jesus said – that it was sick people
who needed a doctor, not healthy people.

> 'Sick, strange, helpless, and lame people are
> signs that a church is really alive. We mustn't
> just tolerate them, we must welcome them.
> That's going to take a lot of self-denial and
> we middle-class churches will only grow if
> we practise it. 'Rocky' questions our lifestyle
> and I'm grateful to people like him who make
> me ask questions of myself. They need to
> find shelter with us on their journey to God.
> We've got to learn to live our lives in such a
> way that the gulf between us doesn't stay
> intolerably wide. Feeling watched is difficult
> for broken people. You can't just be pally
> with an addict. You have to learn to love him,
> to enjoy being with him, to suffer with him
> and to be a brother to him.'

> *Gerhard's pastor – Dietrich Ehl*

So the church learnt to celebrate with every
victory that Jesus won in my life. They were
pretty shocked to meet such a needy person as
me but even more gob-smacked by the way God's
power was reaching the depths of my need.
Children from the church even told my story to
their "enlightened" teachers to prove that God
could still bring dead people back to life today!

I desperately needed people's company and sought it in places where there'd been little warmth before. It seemed to set off a chain reaction. Members of the church began to treat each other differently. People started to invite each other round to their houses more often and got to know each other more deeply. I might have come from a long way outside the church and probably made all the wrong moves but I could see how people felt challenged in what they did and in what they didn't do, about things they'd never thought of before. It was like their rough edges were being knocked off. I laughed when I heard the story of Rahab from Joshua 2:8–21. She was a prostitute, but she helped God's people. So I helped this group of believers to move forward – and they helped me.

Set free

One day in August 1985 I heard that there was going to be a baptism in a month's time. I'd been thinking about being baptised for some time. I'd been free of drugs for a few weeks by then. I didn't hate any more. I felt like I could hide myself away with God.

But before I got baptised I wanted to clear up a few things from my past. I visited the pastor who'd taken in rockers in Cuxhaven and I asked him to forgive me for only ever finding fault with him and never with myself. The pastor said he wanted to ask my forgiveness too, because he'd not come after me when he knew I was crying for help. We prayed together, taking our guilt to the cross of Jesus.

Then I visited an old woman who I'd once got some money from. She'd been too afraid to ask for it back and had written the money off. It was a shock to be reminded just how much power I'd had over people until a short time ago.

Now I wanted to be baptised into the body of Christ and somehow seal my new life. I wanted to give myself completely to Jesus. I said that in the speech I made before I was baptised. I wanted to cut myself off from my old life in which I was the boss. I didn't want to give sin an inch of room now that I'd discovered how good life is with Jesus.

On 1st September 1985 I was finally baptised. I made my renunciation like the people who were baptised in the early church: "I renounce the Evil One and all his works". I was overwhelmed by the joy of being set free even before the actual act of baptism. The few metres from the first row of seats in the church up to the baptistry seemed like miles. It was like my whole life came back before my eyes again. The baptism itself was knock out. I felt a peace and a freedom inside me that were out of this world.

I got a baptism verse. You can find it in Psalm 34:5–6. "I turned to the Lord and he answered me: he freed me from all my fears. Those who look to the Lord, their faces will shine with joy."

The whole church got involved in my baptism celebration. Lots of people knew that I'd used my last cash to pay off all my debts before I got baptised, so they gave me boxes of groceries, stamps and money as presents as well as the usual books.

I'd started a new life. The very next day I went round to the Turkish neighbour I'd hated before and tried to show him the new love I had in my heart. It was the first time I felt free to own up to my past life as well as my new one.

Rocky is dead

It was a big surprise to find that I got angry just as often as I had before. I thought all the evil had been drowned in the water when I was baptised. Could some of it swim? True, I now had different ways to deal with my destructive thoughts. But why did they keep coming back?

I went on a week's "Discipleship School" and on the journey there I met a bloke who'd been a Christian a long time. I told him about this experience. What he told me alarmed me. You see, at my baptism they'd said "Rocky is dead. Gerhard is now alive in Jesus". That was true. But this man told me that it wasn't just Rocky who had to die. Gerhard had to die too, every day. I figured that would take some practice because dying isn't easy!

But for Christians, he said, death is followed by the joy of resurrection. Soon I would begin to have this joy, and people would be able to see that the crucified and risen Jesus had won the victory in my life. It's one thing to say this with your lips: it's another thing for the whole of your body to show that God is at work. The trip was almost worth it just for this one conversation.

My bone cancer had been halted. But in other ways I was still dying. Again and again old wounds were broken open. There were things in my life that God had forgiven me for long ago but which had left scars that now needed healing. How can you go on living with scars like that?

Bit by bit God took me back through all the hurts and guilty corners of my life. As he put his finger on each painful memory, he used it as an opportunity to speak to me. My fifty years of wasted existence turned into a thousand chances to get to know God. And he taught me to recognise the unspoken cries for help of my old mates on St Pauli.

I hung up all my leather gear, my old jacket with the long fringes and hundreds of studs. I gave it to Hans who spends every Saturday night on St Pauli talking about Jesus with the prostitutes and pimps. He was the one who'd helped me take that decisive step.

Hans wears my old jacket as a way in to talking with people on the notorious Herbert Street and the surrounding discos of Hamburg's red light district. The combat boots that went with it were too big for him. So, wearing my gear he went to a shoe shop that sold stuff like that. He was standing in the doorway looking at a picture of me that was hanging on the wall when one of the shop assistants cried out "Hey, that's Rocky's jacket!"

She was dead surprised.

A customer asked "What's up with him then?"

Hans told them Rocky was dead! The shop assistants and the customers acted really shocked.

"Ah, we were afraid of that . . . He was one of the best . . . He was one of us – and now he's gone!"

Hans interrupted their somewhat emotional display of grief.

"But Gerhard is alive. He's been raised from the dead!"

At a charity concert in Hamburg

At my baptism

The whole shop looked at him like a nutter. Was he drunk?

Hans laughed at their reaction. He told them what was really "up" with me. And that really shocked them.

A few weeks later they discovered what Hans meant, when I walked through the Reeperbahn again.

9

Cancer Returns

OK, so God may have healed my screwed-up emotions, but I soon found myself having to handle a whole lot of pain in my body. The cancer was on the move again, and I wound up back in hospital. Perhaps I wasn't quite healed after all. It looked like God had only done half the job.

Then it dawned on me. Maybe the sickness didn't come from God but was the devil's way of trying to tempt me. But even so, God would still know all about it. He wasn't going to leave me on my own even in this last stage of the cancer. So I agreed to have chemotherapy.

If someone had told me before that I had to have this kind of treatment I'd have packed my bags and gone. I wouldn't have had the guts to go through with it. But I couldn't run away from it when God was with me. I didn't want to. He would be my doctor.

When I got readmitted to the hospital they asked me the name of my next of kin. Well, I didn't have a "next of kin", so I gave them the names of my brothers and sisters at the church.

The hospital staff didn't take me seriously. The nurses decided to take special care of me because I was all on my own. After all, it wasn't every day they had someone famous on their ward. But I didn't really need that kind of moral support. The church was supporting me in prayer, and day after day brothers and sisters came to visit me. There were always fresh flowers and fresh fruit by my bedside. And even elderly women from the church with sticks and crutches or in wheelchairs weren't slow in coming to the hospital to pray with me and ask God to heal me.

They didn't always have a lot to say. They didn't have to. And the pastor said he came wanting to bring me lots of things, but in fact went away happier than he came. We had great times together, talking and praying. God was very good. People who came seemed to get as much out of it as I did. The staff were amazed. Even the hospital chaplain was bowled over when he saw such a lively bunch of Christians. I was looked after better than some of the patients who had sons and daughters or other relatives to visit them.

Shared house

When I left hospital I wanted to move into a shared house with other Christians. I found my old flat oppressive. Even the walls had begun to speak to me and tell me the old stories of Rocky the Mohican. I couldn't bear being continually reminded of my past. What's more, the cancer had made me weak. I'd lost the strength even to open a cupboard door. So I asked some church members to wind up the flat for me.

I went straight from hospital to live with some other blokes in a house. I knew the house well, because I'd gone there every morning to "Pray for Hamburg" meetings. I wanted to live with other Christians, to tell people what I'd discovered, and to learn more with my Christian brothers. I found I was able to help some people too, because I'd been to rock-bottom myself. I knew what it was like and I had a kind of understanding for the washed-up people my flat-mates brought in off the streets. Because I'd been healed myself I was

At a mission event

able to help people who were still messed up. And I found God gave me the strength to be available for other people when they needed me. I may not have been able to do very much but I look at it this way: a small stone can make a lot of ripples, especially where God's concerned.

No haloes

I'm not saying everything was always hunky-dory while I was living in the house with the others. It wasn't – not by a long way. We weren't perfect, and we didn't pretend to be. It didn't take a lot of Brasso to polish our haloes! We were so different as people that it was a wonder we could put up with each other at all. We often got on each other's nerves. But every heated discussion brought us a bit closer together. A day didn't go by without one of us having to die a bit in order to live a bit more. We prayed together every day without fail and asked for each other's forgiveness. And it was really important to have the support of other church members.

I'm sure that your life doesn't have to be messed up before it can be changed. Young people can make a fresh start in building their lives by taking the message of the Bible seriously. I'm concerned for young people. And you don't have to grow old before you can start again, you know.

I have a dream for the future. I want to see a house where young people who are homeless and hopeless and who are still a million miles away from knowing Jesus can be taken on board in a loving environment. A house like that would be far cheaper and more effective than any local authority "rehab". But I guess time is running out for me to make that dream come true.

The two Bernds

Let me tell you about a couple of the lads who came to stay at our house. As a matter of fact they were both called Bernd.

Bernd the first was an alcoholic punk. He was in his early twenties. He stayed put in our shared house because he found that Christianity wasn't just talked about; it was put into practice. He was getting medical help, but with us he got love and human companionship too. He was curious to know about "Rocky", of course. When he first arrived he thought I must have gone completely barmy and was playing the saint now. But that impression didn't last long . . . not when he saw what was really going on!

Then there was Bernd the second, another punk in his early twenties. He didn't know anything about my "Rocky" past. He arrived in the house drunk one day and we took him in. He found he was treated with love and understanding. My conversations with Bernd were more than just skin-deep. So he forgot about my tattoos; what was in my eyes was more important. I understood what Bernd was talking about. You see, despite all the heavy experiences I'd had there were so many positive things in my life now. I guess Bernd sensed this, and he started to trust me.

It took a while. At first he was suspicious. He wondered if all this show of concern was just a means to an end. But I didn't put him under any pressure. I didn't hit him over the head with the Bible or anything. I just lived out my new-found way of life.

Some people, I know, are all sympathy when it comes to dealing with the lousy experiences of damaged young people. They never want to say "You're wrong". But a bunch of do-gooding humanist ideals wouldn't have helped this guy.

More than once I left him stone-drunk in his room. There was nothing I could do with him in that state anyway. He was still in the process of drying out when I took him to his first church service. Not that he understood much of it. He blocked the aisle for two hours, standing there in his leathers and chains and black make-up. He wanted to provoke the congregation. In his own way he was showing that he was carrying such a load that he didn't reckon I could handle it alone. But there and then he started to ask God to forgive him, even if he couldn't admit it to other people yet.

"Yeah God, if you exist, God, if you're really there . . ."

We were patient with Bernd and we didn't make demands on him. Step by step he started to trust us. Then he grabbed at the chance to start life over again. One Easter morning he gave his life to God, using some words he'd learnt by heart:

> Father, I give myself to you.
> Do whatever you want with me.
> I'm ready for anything,
> I'll accept everything,
> Just do what you want with me.

"Amen, amen," the church members added, amazed. After Bernd's chain-banging demonstration not many of them had expected to hear him say that.

Today Bernd is at a Discipleship Training School. Soon he'll be working to bring the next lot of people out of the St Pauli drug scene into the light.

*   *   *

When the church and the red-light district collide in a person like me funny things can happen. One day an audibly-drunk man rang up from the Victoria Bar on St Pauli using the telephone number that I'd left there. He got Heinz on the phone. The guy was boasting in a good-humoured way about being my blood-brother and saying that he wouldn't have anything said against me, and then he asked to speak to me. But he also wanted to know who the hell was on the other end of the blower. Heinz told him in a matter-of-fact way that he was my brother too. "Ahh!" said the man, babbling on happily, "then you're one of us. You must be from the red-light district, too." I think Heinz had a different sort of "brother" in mind!

Back to school

The most important bits of my new life in the house were the ordinary bits – quite unspectacular. No-one got special treatment – not even a former pop star like me. No-one was boss over anyone else. We all made our mistakes and we all tried to put them right, starting with ourselves. Rule number one was to look out for each other.

Whenever we started anything, whether it was a party or a job we had to do, we always started with a prayer and a Bible reading. This was the daily routine which everyone agreed to before they moved into the house. Of course, it was never as easy to put into practice as people might have thought when they signed on the dotted line. Good intentions aren't enough. It was a good job that daily prayer and Bible reading were compulsory or we'd never have got round to them.

A month after Bernd had given his life to Christ I was invited into several classes at the local school. Some people in the church had been praying regularly for the school for ten years. They saw my visit as an answer to their prayers. I already had a fan club in the school because I'd visited before when "Rocky" was alive and kicking. Then we'd talked about the prejudice there is against people with tattoos and the reasons why people get themselves tattooed. But now I was speaking to them as a Christian. I tell you, I was shaking inside. But I knew people were praying for me as I went in. It was the kind of school where anything goes when it comes to beliefs. There were teachers who were into transcendental meditation, hypnosis, divining, tarot cards and all sorts of other weird stuff. So I was really glad for the chance to speak to the kids about my new life. Some of them said that despite the old tattoos I looked different now. I was really chuffed at that.

One of the classes I went into had a name in the school for being disruptive. But when I went to speak to them they hung on my every word for a whole hour and a half. You could have heard a pin drop – more like in church than a school classroom. I think the kids liked the fact that I wasn't teaching them stuff out of a text book but was telling them about real life. I took them seriously and tried to start where they were at. Even when I was with the ten-year-olds I tried to treat them as equals, which I think they appreciated.

There was a real buzz when I walked in . . . then they all went dead quiet. They watched every move I made. I don't think they'd ever been so close to someone famous. I told them that everybody needs to have something to lean on as they go through life so that they can get along without falling. I told them a bit about myself and about my own fall and how thankful I was that

In a school lesson surrounded by the kids

God has provided us with someone we can lean on. I told them about Jesus and how he came to show us God's love for us.

Masks

I talked to the tenth class about the masks that we hide behind, all of us, whether teachers, pupils or rockers at the Kiez. I told them how I'd had my own mask tattooed on, how I'd wanted to be a different person, someone that people were afraid of. I told them how God had looked for me and recognised me in spite of my mask and how he'd taken away my fear. Because that was the real truth. I'd been the one with the most to fear. And now my mask was etched on. I couldn't take it off. But I *had* become a different person, a new person with a new heart and a new spirit. One of the teachers left the class in tears.

Then I sang them a song I'd written called "The Mask". I wanted to get it released by the end of 1986:

The Mask

I don't look like other people,
But that's OK.
Why can't you understand,
A word I say?

I've got to wear my mask,
It's here to stay.
When I show you your mask,
You run away.

You say I wear a mask,
What about you?
Perhaps you think you're better,
You wear one too.

I may not have a pretty face,
The latest style.
But if people look and stare at me,
I look and smile.

You think you have to wear a mask,
But God can see.
He'll see right through the mask you wear,
He'll set you free.

I told them straight that becoming a Christian wasn't sudden, like switching a light on. Not for me, anyway. It was like a learning process that went on all through life. Lots of the kids had been mouthing off about God being dead and Jesus being just a fairy story. But now they started laying some heavy questions on me. I held out to answer them for as long as I could. But I tell you it was only God that kept me going through that day at school because I didn't have any strength of my own.

A teacher's view

His skin told one story but his eyes told another. He gave off a real warmth. You couldn't see it at first because we're programmed to have certain expectations of someone who looks like that. I suppose at first we expected him to be a loud-mouthed, extrovert sort of character. But when he talked about his radical change of life it made you think again. We were obviously sceptical at first. I mean we wondered if the way he'd changed was just a new mask, like a new role to play. But it was his eyes that really convinced us. When you saw his eyes you could believe what he was telling you. His face still had the marks of all the terrible things that had happened to him, but behind all that he glowed with a sort of warmth and security.

Maybe the teacher sensed that this security didn't come from me but from somewhere else. If she'd really listened to what I'd said she'd have understood where it came from.

Impressions

After that, lots of the teachers and parents invited me to their homes. If they were expecting the extrovert "Rocky" they got a surprise. I tended to listen a lot and not say much. Sometimes I just sat in silence with people, and that was OK too. For decades my whole life had revolved around me. When I met a stranger they would just stare at me in astonishment. Now I began to get to know people as friends. One of the people I visited came with me to a mission event and became a Christian.

Loads of young people were challenged to think again because I'd visited them. Some pupils wrote me postcards, rang me up and visited me:

> When I saw Rocky for the first time it was weird. I just kept thinking: what's going on inside a person like that? I didn't have an answer but I wanted to keep my distance, like everyone else did. But when he came into our class one day and told us about himself I was sorry for how I'd reacted because I realised it wasn't his fault that he'd got into drugs before and got violent. I guess everyone always took him for a violent person so he just slipped into the role that everyone was pushing him into.
>
> *Christine (14)*

I used to be like the people that Rocky hung around with. Now I know that it's only the inside of a person that matters. I believe that Gerhard is massive proof of the fact that, even if you've sunk really low, the way to God is still open to you. Even now that he's ill he must be happy inside because he's on his way to God.

Sara (15)

I never suspected what would come out of my meeting with Rocky and how it would change my life. The first time I saw what he looked like I thought "Man! That's dangerous!" But when I was able to speak to him I found he was quite different inside. Even though he was ill himself he was getting involved with other sick people. He was a man who'd found strength from God, and this world could do with more of it. He could talk to anyone because he's seen a lot of life.

Sven (17)

Back on my old patch

In May 1986 I walked across the Reeperbahn again. I hadn't been there for a year, and it was the first time I'd been there not wearing my leathers. I went into the infamous Elbschlosskeller bar. Friends from the old days hailed me drunkenly. They couldn't get over the "Jesus lives" sticker on my lapel.

"You what? Jesus lives? You can't be serious?"

"Sure I'm serious," I said with a grin "or I wouldn't be wearing it."

When they realised I meant it they weren't sure where they stood with me.

"Do you still want to know us then? Are you still going to come round here?"

I was stunned by their questions. Was there really such a big gulf between the church and the Kiez? If so, then there was a gulf between God's people and the very people that Jesus had died for.

"What d'*you* think?!" I said. "Let's get this straight. I really love you lot!"

I talked to them about the way I'd discovered God's love. I wasn't tongue-tied at all. I told them all about Jesus – that he was alive and that he loved all of them too . . . if only they would let him.

The festival

In June 1986 schoolteacher Mike Ackermann and I were invited to the "Dünenhof Festival" in Berensch near Cuxhaven. It was put on every year by a group of people called "The Companions". "The Companions" were a community of fifteen young Christians, families and single people, who lived together to work for Christ. One part of their work was to run a big retreat centre near Cuxhaven where this festival took place. There were lots of other well-known Christian speakers invited as well.

While we were waiting on the station platform in Hamburg I felt so weak that I didn't know whether I would make it as far as Cuxhaven. I propped myself up against the wall and Mike prayed for me. The nearer we got to Cuxhaven the more strength I seemed to get back. By the time the evening came I didn't need to hold on to the sofa that had been put on the stage for me. I stood at the microphone for nearly two hours. Mike could hardly believe his eyes.

There were about two hundred young people in the audience. They had no time for conversion stories. They'd heard it all before. But, perhaps because of that, lots of them were deeply moved by what I had to say. They'd never seen a conversion so radical or with such obvious consequences.

I really wanted to leave after the first evening but I ended up speaking on the next three nights. I had so much I wanted to say to the young people. I met lots of them afterwards. Sometimes people came in pairs, sometimes in groups. I had to find the strength for up to thirty conversations a night.

On the first night I had a surprising visit from a fifty-year-old man. He came straight up to me and asked me to forgive him. I was a bit puzzled. Then he explained:

"Ten years ago I saw you on Tal Street at St Pauli. I was in my Salvation Army uniform at the

At the Dünenhof Festival

time and when I saw what a rough-looking character you were I prayed to God to keep you away so that you wouldn't disturb our open air service. I could hardly believe it when I realised you were the same man. And there you were standing up in front of me, speaking with all the power of the resurrected Christ. I could tell you were speaking by God's power because it's obvious that physically you're in a bad way. I've been listening to you all evening and thanking God again and again for what I've been seeing and hearing. Then I thought about what might have happened if I'd told you about Jesus ten years earlier and you'd believed in him then. It left me feeling really guilty. So I told God about it in a prayer and now I've come up to tell you."

*   *   *

Young people whose families had been Christians for generations recognised in talking to me that being a fifty per cent or even an eighty per cent Christian wasn't much cop. In fact it's pretty useless. To be a Christian is a hundred per cent thing. It isn't just about teaching in the Sunday school, going to church and saying grace before meals.

At the closing service on Bank Holiday Monday I said a prayer for the people at the festival and for "The Companions". I prayed that they would grow like only God can make you grow. He gives people real power.

*   *   *

Gerhard is an extraordinary bloke. He's got some likeable idiosyncracies. I guess they're left over from his father's influence. When we were at the Dünenhof festival I got to know some of them. At six o'clock in the morning he'd transform our room into a Prussian army barracks. He'd wake me up as if he was a sergeant major.

"Michael, the reading for the day!"

I'd rouse myself from sweet slumber, grab my Bible reading notes and my Bible, and read. Afterwards, in a booming General's voice, he would thank God for His word and for the new morning and then, whilst I retreated back under the bedclothes, he would concentrate on dyeing his moustache and styling his hair!

Mike Ackermann – schoolteacher

Serving God from a hospital bed

A few days after we got back from Cuxhaven I was rushed back into Altona hospital. One of my lungs had been completely eaten away and the other was only working at twenty per cent. The cancer in my stomach had gone wild. I was so weak I could hardly open my bedside drawer. In one way I was nearly finished. But you know in other ways this is where things really started for me.

Even though I guessed I was on my death-bed God had powerful plans. He used me to help other people to find life. There was a punk girl who held my hand with tears streaming down her face. Her eyes were heavy with black make-up. I was very weak, but we had a wonderful conversation. I was close to death, but she was just coming alive. And the following day a fifteen-year-old boy came in. His teachers had decided they couldn't get through to him at all. Poor lad, he just couldn't cope with the steady stream of men his mother brought back home with her. Some of them were not much older than he was. I knew the club where his mother hung out. I knew the scene there, what went and what didn't, so I got her to come in and talk to me.

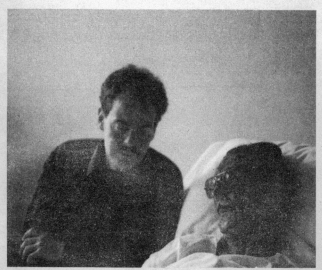

Mike Ackermann visiting me in hospital

Another pupil used to come in every week. He was only seventeen but he was on heroin. We used to pray together. I think it was the first time he'd found someone who could understand him.

The news that I was back in hospital hit some of the kids quite hard. Some of them wrote to me. They even wrote me poems. I bet they wouldn't have done that for their teachers!

Rockers' reunion

About a week later I got a phone call at the hospital. It was Elli Pirelli, a rocker from Udo's Panik Crew.

"Rocky," she said, "what do you think about life after death?"

I answered her gently: "That's when life really takes off!"

Three weeks later she rang again. She told me openly that she knew now that real power comes from God. Before she put the phone down she said:

"I hope I'll see you again Rocky; but next time you won't be in pain. You'll be dressed in new clothes, standing next to Jesus in all his glory."

We were both in tears by this time. She talked about how meaningless life had become for her, going from one tour to the next, one show to the next. An endless round of gigs and travel.

"Funny," she said. "The real discoveries happen in the quiet times, and often when you're down."

We'd both known how meaningless life could be. We both knew what it was to hit rock-bottom.

Shortly after this phone call the door opened and a man in black leathers walked up to my bedside. It was Klaus, a rocker from my early days in the gang scene. He'd tracked me down through old acquaintances in Hamburg. He had no idea what had happened to me since we last met.

We were over the moon to see each other again. Klaus asked me whether I was still on heroin. I told him straight that I'd found something better. He was all ears. He wanted to know about the new "stuff". I told him the "stuff" was the healing love of Jesus. Klaus couldn't really make out what I was on about, but he said he wanted to come again and hear some more.

Udo Lindenberg asked his tour doctor about me. Udo knew I'd found something that made me peaceful and it was something he was looking for himself.

I went on the hospital radio, which gave me a chance to thank everyone for the loving care they'd shown me. And I prayed on the air for God's blessing and courage for the patients on all fifteen floors.

More and more people came in – and not just people who needed help. I think they sensed that I could understand how people had got into the situations they were in.

A schoolboy brought his sceptical father in to meet me. He had cancer too and he'd been through a divorce. The man came again by himself. The radiation treatment had taken its toll by this time and I could only manage to whisper to him about God's love.

A Sunday school teacher from a neighbouring church came to ask me for advice, clutching a bunch of flowers. She was eighteen. She said she'd been brought up in a strict religious home by parents who were very protective towards her. And now her mother was dying of cancer. I couldn't hold back the tears as we spoke.

"We have to learn to let go," I told her. "It's only then that we learn to live."

It's simple, but it's true. I hope you will learn it in time.

10

More Visitors

Since her mother died, the Sunday school teacher has kept on coming to see me every week to pray with me and to find the strength to go back home and look after her lonely dad. Often she goes home with tears of relief in her eyes. She brought some of her friends one day and then they started bringing their friends. Now more and more visitors are coming here to the hospital to see me in my "mission-bed"! All sorts of people meet up here at my bedside – people who would never meet any other way: there are people from the red-light district, from show business, from the rock scene and the gay clubs, meeting up with people who've been Christians for decades. People come with loads of questions. Some of the contacts made at my bedside don't end here. Elli Pirelli is often on the phone to church members. Some people find new faith which will last long after I'm gone. Others take steps forward in their faith.

Pupils from Mike Ackermann's class have started to bring their parents in with them. After the usual talk about tattoos, the conversation goes on to more important things. Parents who are ill or divorced have big questions, and they want better answers than they get from most people.

On 26th November 1986 I celebrated my sixtieth birthday here in the hospital. You should have seen the number of visitors and cards! The nurses came round with a cream cake loaded with burning candles. Singers from Youth with a Mission came and sang about their faith in the ward. I couldn't stop talking about how good God had been to me.

Not long after my birthday the Christian writer Günther Klempnauer visited me to do an interview with Mike and me. He wanted to make a programme to go out on West German Radio and Transworld Radio the following March.

"You seem so close to God. You seem to have such a simple relationship with him," he said. "Would you doubt God if you didn't get better?"

I thought for a while and then said, "No. I just pray 'Lord, do what you want.' I've reached a stage where I've completely let go of my life. Of course, I've said to God, 'If there's anything else I can do for you then I'd love to, if you can give me time.' But I would just as happily fall asleep now and go to him because I know that's where the light is. God has been so kind to me in the course of this year and blessed me more than I can say."

A few days later Klempnauer played the tape to Fritz Rau, Europe's greatest rock promoter, who knew me as "Rocky". He was very moved by

what he heard and quizzed Klempnauer about
how the change in me had come about.

*   *   *

I look quite gaunt now. My body has wasted
away. My trademark, my Mohican haircut, has
gone. All my hair has fallen out. The remaining
signs of my old life are increasingly losing their
effect. I am even more determined to follow Jesus
right to the end. I don't mind that the end is
coming. After all, I've had two whole years of
living in the light. I just want to carry on growing in my faith and being a strength to other
people.

*   *   *

Just before Christmas Gerhard was taken from
the main hospital to the Tabea rest home in
Hamburg-Nienstedten. The doctors couldn't do
anything more for him. At the same time the book
of his life was published: *Rocky – the Man with the
Mask*. The Sunday before Christmas, Hans,
who'd first talked to Rocky at Altona Station,
stood up at the front of the church and asked
people to buy copies of the book so that he could
give them to people at the Kiez. A hundred and
fifty people bought the book and pressed their
copies into his hands.

It was like a grenade going off on the Reeperbahn. Pimps and prostitutes left the bars to go
and read Rocky's book undisturbed. They shut

up shop. Some people rejected what they read about. They didn't want anything to do with it. Other people began to ask questions. One woman who ran a tattoo parlour said she would sell the book. A croupier from one of the gambling dens went into a Christian bookshop for the first time in her life and furtively asked for Rocky's book. She ended up talking to the assistant about her memories of Rocky.

Meanwhile, Gerhard had become so weak that his voice had shrunk to a whisper. The stream of visitors still went on. If anything, it became even more colourful: a Swiss sociology lecturer, a gay bouncer from St Pauli, school-children, elderly ladies from the church. Most of them had never seen someone whom God had changed so much.

January 1987

After the New Year Gerhard's condition deteriorated badly. The old Rocker-Kommandant, who'd once been so violent, looked completely calm. His expression was innocent – almost child-like. The last time he prayed with us he simply said, ''Father, I'm coming to you.'' As we left he waved us goodbye. It was as if he was leaving the stage for the last time. On the morning of 4th January 1987 Gerhard Bauer didn't wake up.

Two Hamburg newspapers ran major features on his life and death. People from the Kiez cried openly. Many people there had loved his gentleness and his sensitivity, especially towards women. But we at the church couldn't mourn. Gerhard was with God. Jesus's victory was complete. When the news of his death was announced to the church we sang the song "The steadfast love of the Lord never ceases".

On 15th January nearly two hundred Christians and a hundred other friends from St Pauli, the gay and showbiz scene, neighbours and curious teenagers – people who had never set foot in a church – all came together. The chapel at the cemetery wasn't big enough for the farewell celebrations. Gerhard's coffin was carried by church members. The funeral service became a chance to proclaim the good news about Jesus. We sang joyful songs of victory and the pastor spoke about the Prodigal Son who returned home. He told the mourners that Gerhard hadn't looked for God, but God had gone after Gerhard because he loved him, and had brought him home.

A police escort led the way to the ceremony. As we gathered beside the open grave it was freezing – minus fifteen degrees. Even some of the rockers couldn't hide their tears. Two prostitutes whispered to each other:

"Yeah, if you've got faith like that you can die peacefully."

For the first time we realised how much we would miss Gerhard. People went back into the church building together, not wanting to go their separate ways. We were like mosaic stones from Gerhard's life: Theo the tattooist, Elli Pirelli, school-children, punks and others, all sitting round together. That's what Gerhard did for us. Let's keep it that way.

Instead of an Epilogue . . .

Help for the helpers . . . based on an in-depth conversation between Michael Ackermann and Hans from the Jesus Centre who has worked with Rocky, and with people like him, over the past twelve years:

The mask-wearers

Gerhard Bauer's life illustrates so much of the history of Germany in this century. After the First World War the country lay in tatters. Fascism grew rapidly as a brutal consequence. These factors dictated Gerhard's early years. He was the child of a Nazi official growing up in a socialist, working-class area of Berlin, the capital of the old régime. The defeat of the Third Reich cost Gerhard his father and his home. What might have been a reconciling union between the son of a Nazi and the daughter of a conscientious objector could not survive the politics of the divided Germany.

In the Bautzen prison camp Gerhard saw East Germany with its mask off. And it wasn't long before he saw through the mask of West Germany's "economic miracle" too. He saw how minority groups, and particularly people with a disability, were treated as second

*class citizens. Then in his involvement with the drop-
outs of society Gerhard faced the hard reality that even
amongst the punks and the rockers there were "rules"
in operation – rules that often outdid the brutality of
respectable society.*

*Loneliness, lack of identity and hatred of other people
reached their worst excesses in the world of show
business and in the rock scene around Udo Lindenberg.
Gerhard was on a slippery slope. He was only stopped
by a chance meeting with a group of quite traditional
Christians. They didn't just stand in judgement. They
rolled up their sleeves and got involved with him.*

*Gerhard himself said, "Most people don't really
believe the things they claim to believe, or at least they
don't act like it." These people did.*

*Christianity that was limited to meeting socially and
being nice to each other wouldn't have been adequate to
change the life of a rocker like Gerhard Bauer. Only the
power of the risen Christ in people's lives can do that.*

Hard questions

*When you read Gerhard's story, when you look him in
the face, you have to decide how to respond. Are you
prepared to open yourself to people like him? To say no
would be a slap in the face for Gerhard Bauer. It would
be a slander to the man, his story and his breakthrough
into life.*

*Whether you're on the left or the right, a non-believer
or a church-goer you have to meet the challenge. Anyone who has wholeheartedly given themselves to Jesus
will be amazed and overjoyed at the greatness of our*

You have to understand that everybody's the same underneath . . . We're just human beings

God. He works miracles in the lives of the very people
we have most given up on. He reached Rocky when,
according to our watches, it was already ten past
midnight.

But who knows God's timescale? He dealt with the
lost son in his own time. He needed a couple of street
artists, a couple of disciples who weren't prejudiced and
who would make themselves available to be used by him.

It was complete acceptance with no strings attached
that brought Gerhard into the church and into God's
family. The love of God is based on this unconditional
acceptance. It is the strongest of weapons and it dis-
armed even a man like Rocky. People who were full of
God's love did not let Rocky's appearance shock them.
They left their pride behind. They didn't just see things
as they looked on the outside. God gave them an eye for
the inner conflict of a man whom God himself saw
already healed.

We too can allow God to give us the gift of seeing
through people's masks. With his help we can see into
their hearts as he does (1 Samuel 16:7).

What's needed

Each of us has the potential to love people like Rocky. It
comes with the faith that renews us. It's just that often
we get clogged up by life's concerns so that the living
water of God's love can't flow through us. Disgust,
hatred and the fear of being disturbed can only be
removed by God. And then only if we let him.

This is vital and so relevant for us today. Gerhard
Bauer knew that, and spoke from his own experience:

"Right up to the last days of the war I was dragged along by the mass fanaticism skilfully whipped up by the Nazis: 'The Führer commands. We obey.' It was the same for many young people."

He warned us that the hatred that was directed at the Jews and the Russians then is being mobilised against immigrants today. The form may be different but the danger remains the same. He told us how respectable citizens in his part of town are approaching former army officers for advice in the fight against unwanted minority groups.

"Only Jesus Christ can set us free from the hatred of immigrants, because we learn from him to see foreigners as our brothers," he said.

People who live in the love of God are a puzzle to the rest of society. They can't be pigeon-holed. They cause people to sit up and think. The solution to the puzzle is that God is in them.

People only have to be what they are in God's eyes — his children. Then they experience a peace and security because they know they are accepted by God. Only when you have this security can you help damaged, violent or ruthless people. Everything you need comes from the outpouring of your whole life with Jesus Christ: a complete trust in him, obedience to God, and the faith that he will make something positive out of the most absurd situation.

If we're faithful in the small things of everyday life as if they were big things, then God will give us the grace to do the big things as if they were small. God can take every fear and transform it into love.

On the other hand it is true that those who follow Jesus will suffer persecution. For that reason we put *ourselves daily under the protection of the blood of Jesus and pray: "Lord, make me a person after your own heart."*

False pictures of God

Not every "Rocky" story runs like the one we've just been told. Many damaged people return to their old lives. On the one hand that's certainly the result of Christians who don't live out what they say. On the other hand it may be that the picture many Christians — especially young people — have of God is not a right one. They think God will dance to their tune if only they pray to him. Jesus is allowed to be their Saviour but not their Lord. We let him bless our affairs but not really rule in every part of our life. For many people, faith is reserved for particular times. The old gods are not thrown in the fire: ideals of appearance and beauty, image, business status, standard of living are still important. So they don't hear when Jesus says: "Not everyone who says to me, 'Lord, Lord,' will enter the kingdom of heaven, but only he who does the will of my Father who is in heaven" (Matthew 7:21).

Everyone who has really come to Jesus must be forgiven for making mistakes. Every Christian does at first. Even people who have been Christians a long time still make mistakes and still need forgiveness. But we must also be ready to correct each other in love — giving and receiving.

God's grace

Whoever takes a genuine decision to follow Jesus does not walk in darkness again, even if there are many setbacks and deviations.

Many new converts from a damaged background have doubts because they can't live up to their own expectations of their new life. Very often they can't forgive themselves. They have to come back to the cross many times with the same sins until they can accept that they've really been forgiven.

Sometimes there's a need for more intensive pastoral counselling. More and more people, not just those from Rocky's background, are oppressed by occult practices, perverted sexuality, blasphemous thoughts, the guilt of abortions and so on. All too many pastors send these people to psychologists and doctors even though the only thing that can really bring them inner healing and liberation is a genuine renunciation of all the powers of the Evil One.

Many people rashly suggest that individuals have to earn God's grace. A man like Rocky could never have earned his own forgiveness. But the grace of God is inexhaustible for those who accept it by faith.

We can be reassured that a seed that was potentially a tree had been planted in Gerhard earlier on. It took decades before that life could finally grow in him. Today he's a new creation. The foundation on which Gerhard stands was laid a long time ago by the one who had created him. We have to learn that God's Kingdom isn't like Aladdin's magic lamp!

J John

LIFE MEANS WHAT?

What is life all about? Is there anything beyond the
here and now? Happiness is elusive in the modern
world. Fear, anxiety and loneliness are hallmarks of
our society. Where is the cure? Wealth and possessions do not supply it, any more than fame, brilliance
or good looks. Where else can we look? To God?

TEN STEPS TO THE GOOD LIFE

'The ten commandments are God's irreducible mini-
mum for living. We need to know them and by God's
grace and strength endeavour to live them.' Convinced of the relevance of God's law as given to Moses,
J John examines the ten commandments afresh and
explains what they are all about. Using a fund of
illustrations and stories he shows how the commandments are *Ten Steps to the Good Life*.

John Young

THE CASE AGAINST CHRIST

What keeps people in the Church? Is Christianity worth investigating? In response to such questions, John Young provides a defence of the Christian faith for atheists, agnostics, enquirers, and Christians, offering compelling evidence for the existence of an active and loving God.

'If there is a better book at answering popular objections to the Christian faith, I'd like to see it.'

Reconciliation Quarterly

OUR GOD IS STILL TOO SMALL

What is God like? Examining popular myths and misconceptions about God with humour and insight, John Young shows how our understanding of God has practical implications for the way we live, the way we view the world, and for our peace of mind – or lack of it.

'I think it's a splendid book, racily written, readable and entertaining, yet profound, thought provoking and at times extremely powerful.'

Joyce Huggett